Philographics

BIS Publishers
Building Het Sieraad
Postjesweg 1
1057 DT Amsterdam
The Netherlands

T +31 (0)20 515 02 30
F +31 (0)20 515 02 39
bis@bispublishers.nl
www.bispublishers.nl

Concept and design: Genis Carreras
Original text: Chris Thomas
www.geniscarreras.com

Philographics was self-published by the
author in May 2013. This is the extended
second edition, first published by
BIS Publishers in October 2013.

ISBN 978 90 6369 341 1

Philographics

Big ideas in simple shapes

Genís Carreras

BISPUBLISHERS

About the author

Genis Carreras (Salt, 1987) is a
Catalan born graphic designer
currently living and working in
London, United Kingdom.

As a designer he has worked
for different agencies creating
logos, posters, packaging, book
and album covers for clients
all around the globe including
Sony Music, O2, Ballantine's or
Red Cross. Up to date, his work
has been exhibited in France,
UK, USA, the Netherlands and
Spain, and featured in several
publications.

In his work, Carreras uses
geometry and vibrant colours to
create beautiful and meaningful
pieces. When he's not designing,
Genis enjoys cooking, playing
video games, drinking a good
lager and spending time with
good company in East London
and in Salt.

Introduction

Philographics is conceived as a visual dictionary of philosophy, which depicts the world's most important 'isms' using simple shapes and colour. The project merges the world of philosophy and graphic design, two areas that seem completely opposites: one is heavy and complex, the other eye-catchy and fast-consumed. The result of this blend is a collection of 95 graphics that boil down complex schools of thought, sometimes explained using visual metaphors, others by using existent symbolisms or creating new ones using abstract representations.

The idea came from my last year at University while I was looking for an efficient way to explain philosophy to our generation of visual learners – people with a rather short attention span who struggle to finish the books we buy. Initially, the graphics were designed to go hand-by-hand with essays in order to make them more inviting, but soon I realised that the visual itself could explain part of the concept behind the words and I decided to start the quest to create one graphic for every single 'ism'. Two years later, having worked with more than 100 philosophical theories, I put together all this collection into one single book.

The journey to get this book published wasn't easy and, after a series of events, I decided to self-publish the book with the help of the crowdfunding site Kickstarter. The funding campaign was a huge success, exceeding my initial target by more than 4 times.

Five months later, this extended 2nd edition of the book was first published thanks to BIS Publisher, helping me to bring this collection to you and closing a journey that started almost 3 years ago.

How to use this book

Each theory is explained in two pages: one with the title and a brief definition, and one with the visual representation of the theory. An icon next to the number of the page indicates which branch of philosophy the theory belongs to:

 Methaphysics
(reality, being, and the world)

 Ethics
(right and wrong, good or bad)

 Epistemology
(acquisition of knowledge)

 Politics

 Religion

 Other

Some theories are directly linked to others. This is shown with a grey arrow and a number placed under the page number that indicates where these connections can be found within the book.

The visuals of this book are open to different interpretations, allowing the reader to draw their own path to connect the idea behind each theory with its form. This plurality of points of view reflects all the different theories to see and understand the world that are compiled on this book.

The book aims to be the starting point of deeper discussion about these theories, it's a trigger of conversation to bring philosophy back to our daily lives. Thus, this book is not created to replace the more conventional philosophy books, but to work closely with them.

Philographics will help you to discover new theories that you didn't know that existed, or will make you change the way you perceive those you already knew. I hope you enjoy reading (and watching) my Philographics.

Genís Carreras

Philographics

Absolutism.

The position that within a particular school of thought, all different perspectives are either absolutely true or absolutely false.

8 ◐◑□
→ 162

Absurdism.

The contention that the attempts of man to find meaning in the universe will ultimately fail because no such meaning exists.

Aestheticism.

The belief that our main efforts in life should be focused on creating and enjoying beauty, in all its forms.

Altruism.

The practice and principle of using actions to benefit others, expecting nothing in return.

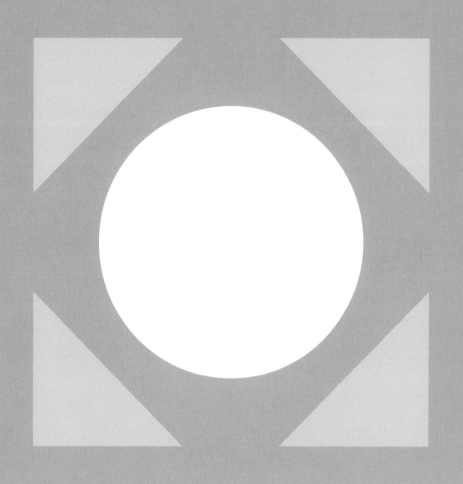

Anarchism.

A range of views that oppose the idea of the state as a means of governance, instead advocating a society based on non-hierarchical relationships.

16 ●
→ 26

Anthropocentrism.

The conviction that the existence of human beings is the central reason for the universe's existence.

Asceticism.

An approach to life typified by restraining from worldly pleasures, in order to pursue a more virtuous or enlightened existence.

Atheism.

The absence of belief that gods or deities exist.

Atomism.

The theory that all things in the universe are composed of very small, indestructible elements.

Authoritarianism.

The organization of society through strong, often oppressive measures against its people.

Capitalism.

An economic system based on the production of goods for profit, and the private ownership of the means of production.

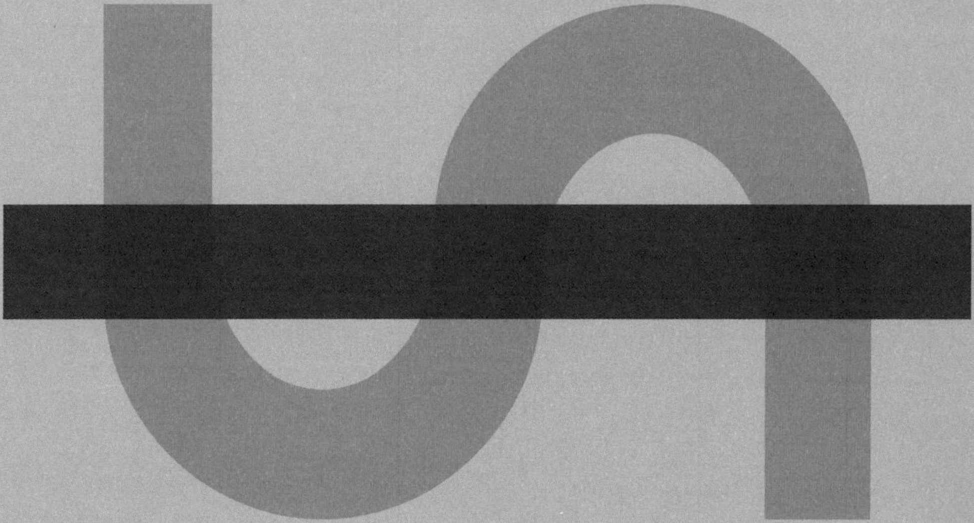

Collectivism.

A view that places emphasis on the group over the individual, often holding the belief that the "greater good" of the group is more important than the good of any individual within it.

30 ●
→ 106

Compatibilism.

The theory that free will and determinism are compatible.
That choices in life could have been made differently had
different circumstances preceded them.

Consequentialism.

The view that the consequences of a potential action or policy are the most important considerations when debating whether or not to go ahead with it.

34 ◓

→ 46

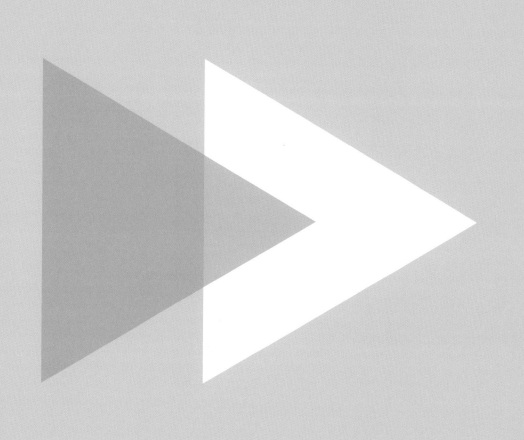

Constructivism.

The view that reality, and the methods we use to understand it, are man-made, subjective constructions rather than an objective reading of events.

36 ☐

→ 42

Contextualism.

A range of views that argue that a phenomenon can only be properly understood within the context it occurred.

Cynicism.

The lack of belief in selfless or sincere human qualities, such as altruism, honesty or virtue, believing instead that people are driven only by self-interest.

Deconstructivism.

A school of thought dedicated to critiquing the assumptions and ideas that form the basis of our understanding of the world.

42 ☐
→ 36

Deductionism.

A view of how scientific knowledge should be acquired –
by first proposing a hypothesis, then attempting to prove it
wrong through empirical tests on observable data.

44 ☐
→ 108

Deontologism.

An ethical system that judges the morality of an action according to its adherence to a set of pre-defined principles, rather than its implications or consequences.

46 ◐

→ 34

Determinism.

The proposition that all events, including those of human thoughts, are causally determined by an unbroken chain of prior events.

48 ▲

→ 88

Dialetheism.

The view that some statements can be true and false at the same time, known as a "true contradiction".

Dogma.

The inflexible adherence to a rigid doctrine or ideology,
not open to rational argument or debate.

Dualism.

The conviction that all concepts within the world fundamentally
consist of two contrasting qualities, such as good and evil,
or body and mind.

→ 122, 148

Dynamism.

The idea that the material world can be understood as active forces, the movement and interaction of which form the basis of all phenomena in the universe.

Eclecticism.

A conceptual approach that does not stick to a single paradigm or set of assumptions, but instead draws upon multiple theories or styles to gain a more varied or balanced insight into something.

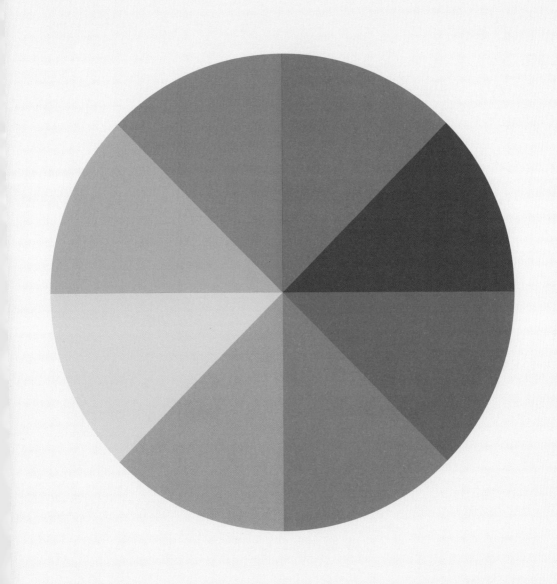

Egalitarianism.

A political ideology that holds that all people should be treated as equals.

Egoism.

The ethical position that conscious beings ought to always do what is in their own self-interest.

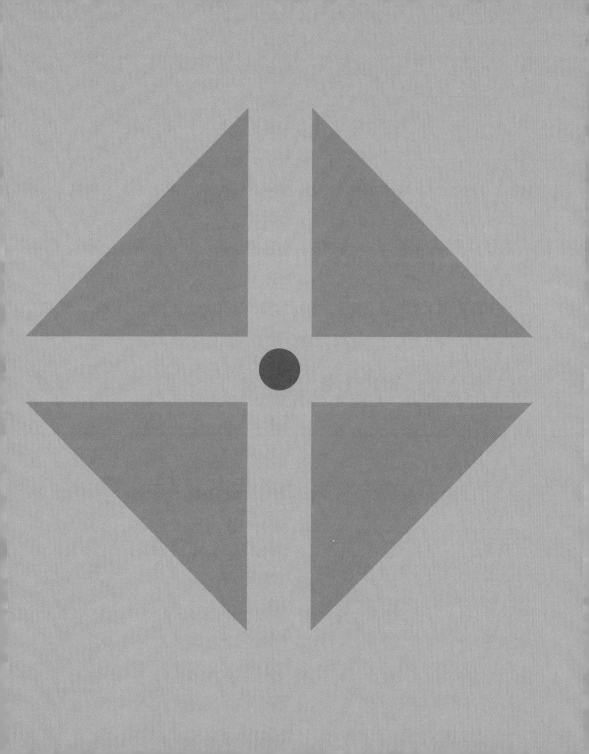

Emotivism.

The assertion that all individual ethical judgements are purely expressions of one's own attitude intended to change the actions or attitudes of others.

Empiricism.

The scientific doctrine stating that all knowledge ultimately comes from sensory experience and observable evidence, rather than intuition or pre-conceived ideas.

66 □
→ 154

Epiphenomenalism.

The view that physical events have effects on mental processes, but that mental processes have no physical effects whatsoever.

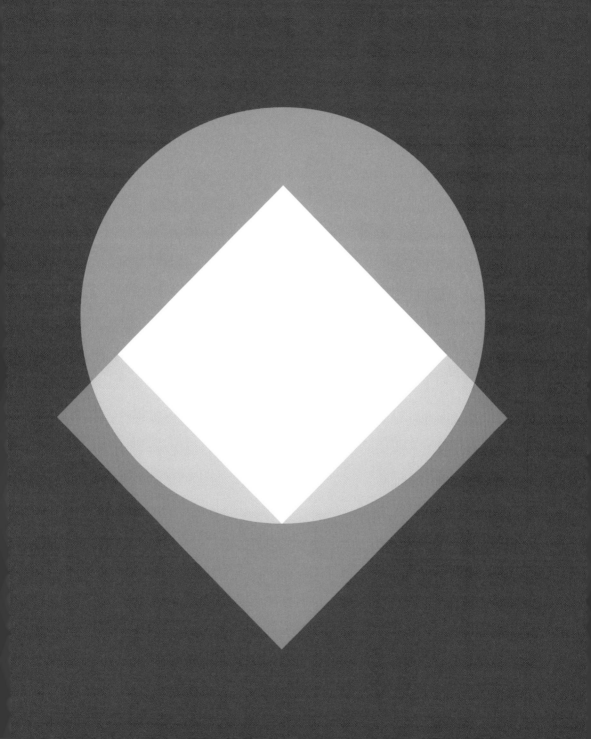

Eternalism.

The philosophical position that time is just another dimension, that future events already exist, and that all points in time are equally real.

Ethnocentrism.

The tendency to view the world with one's own culture
and identity at the center of everything.

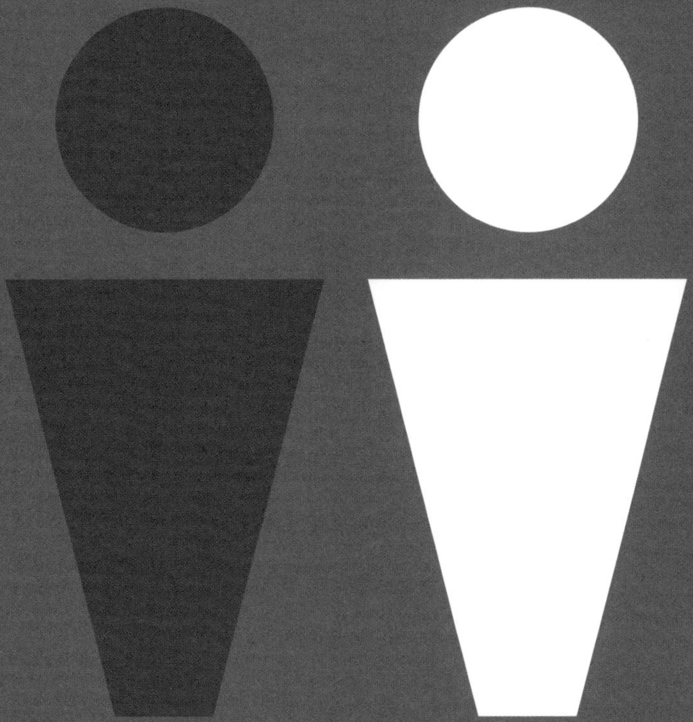

Eudaimonism.

A system of ethics that evaluates actions in terms of their capacity to produce happiness.

Existentialism.

The idea that all philosophical thought must begin with the experiences
of the individual, and it is up to the individual to give meaning
and authenticity to their own existence.

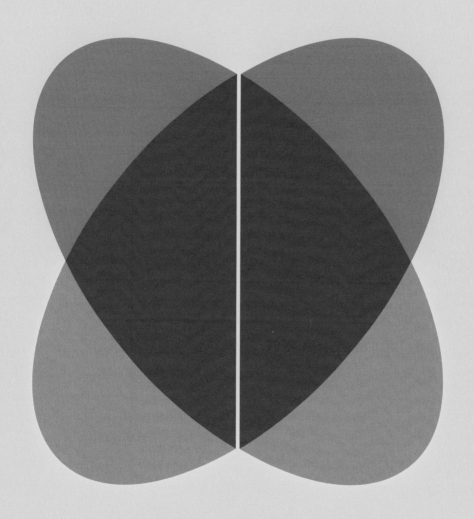

Externalism.

The position that the mind and human experience
is not just the result of the nervous system and brain,
but also the phenomena that exist outside of it.

Extropy.

A system of ethics concerned with negotiating the gradual development of the human condition that is occurring due to advances in technology.

Feminism.

A range of social and moral philosophies concerned with
the experiences of women in society, most often with the intent
of eradicating gender inequality.

Finalism.

The assertion that any event is defined by a pre-set final outcome,
and that all events leading up to that outcome are shaped by it.

Formalism.

The view that in any cultural product, it is the form
rather than the content that provides true meaning.

Free will.

The ability of conscious agents to be free to make their own decisions, free of any social, moral or political constraints.

88 ▲

→ 48

Hedonism.

The ethical position that pleasure is the ultimate goal and greatest good, and should be the central aim of all decisions made.

Historicism.

The theory that to understand a historical event, you must understand
the philosophical context that it took place in, rather than explain it
with supposedly timeless or fundamental ideas.

92 ●
→ 28

Holism.

The theory that the properties of a system cannot be understood by the sum of its parts alone, but by how the system behaves as a whole.

Humanism.

A range of ethical views that consider human nature to be the source of morality.

Hylozoism.

The philosophical theory that all material things possess life,
or that life is inseparable from matter.

Idealism.

The philosophical view that asserts that reality is fundamentally based on, and shaped by, ideas and mental experience, rather than material forces.

Illusionism.

A philosophy that holds that there is no material world but rather a collection of illusions formed by human consciousness that results in an environment that all humans live within.

Indeterminism.

The philosophical belief contradictory to determinism: that there are events that are in some way uncaused.

104 ▲

→ 48

Individualism.

The political stance that the rights of individuals should be protected over that of collectives, such as states, religions or social groups.

Inductivism.

The view that scientific progress is guided by the various observations made in previous experiments, and that statements of truth should be based on this mass of observations.

108 □

→ 44

Innatism.

The belief that the mind is born with ideas and knowledge, rather than learning it as you go through life.

Instrumentalism.

The idea that the truth of knowledge is irrelevant, and that knowledge should be judged by its usefulness.

Legalism.

The strict adherence to a legislative text, such as a constitution, federal law or religious scripture.

Materialism.

The philosophical view that the only thing that can truly be said to 'exist'
is matter; that fundamentally, all things are composed of 'material'
and all phenomena are the result of material interactions.

Mechanicism.

The theory that all natural phenomena can be explained by physical causes, and can be understood through their parts and functions rather than any holistic interpretation.

118 ▲

→ 94

Meliorism.

The idea that humans can, through their interference with natural processes, produce a more desirable outcome than the natural one.

Monism.

The metaphysical and theological view that there is only one principle, essence, substance or energy that forms the basis of all phenomena.

Mysticism.

The pursuit of a state of consciousness or being that profoundly explains or transcends reality.

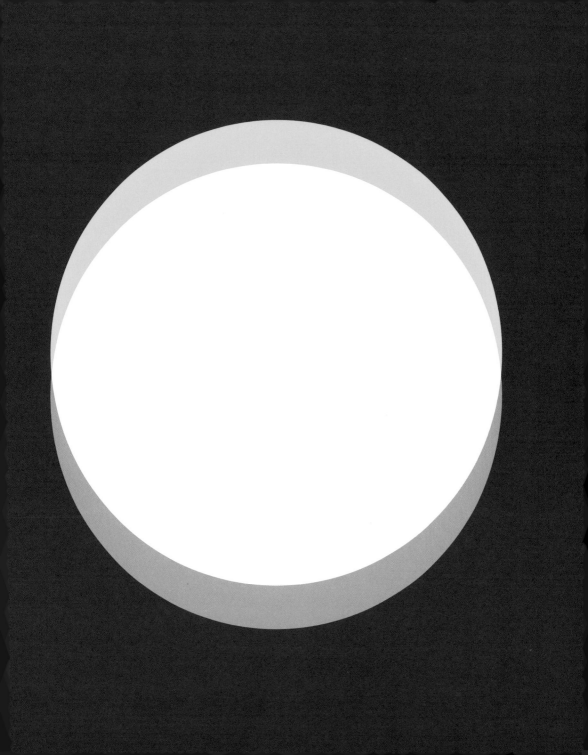

Naturalism.

Range of philosophical stances that do not distinguish
the supernatural from nature, and thus claim that they
can be studied using the same methods.

Nihilism.

The view that the world, and human existence in particular, is without meaning, purpose, truth, or value.

Nominalism.

The belief that universal or mental concepts have no objective reality, and exist only as the words or "names" we give them.

Objectivism.

In ethics, the belief that certain acts can be objectively right or wrong.

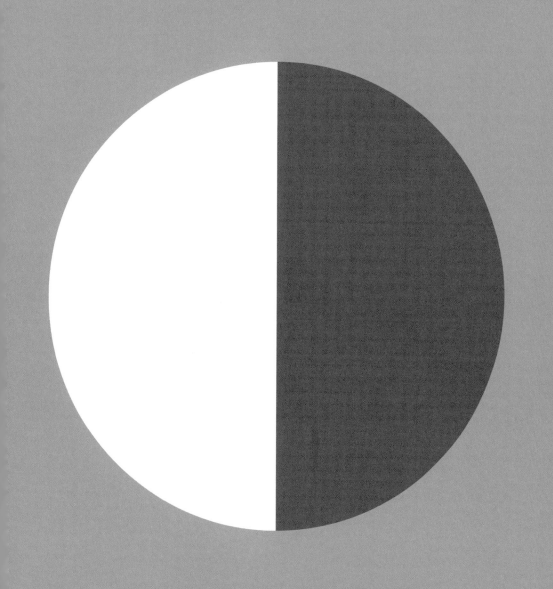

Occasionalism.

A theory denying efficient causation between mundane events, instead believing that all events are caused directly by a God or higher power.

Optimism.

Historically, the philosophical position that this is the best of all possible worlds, more often used to describe a cheerful or positive worldview.

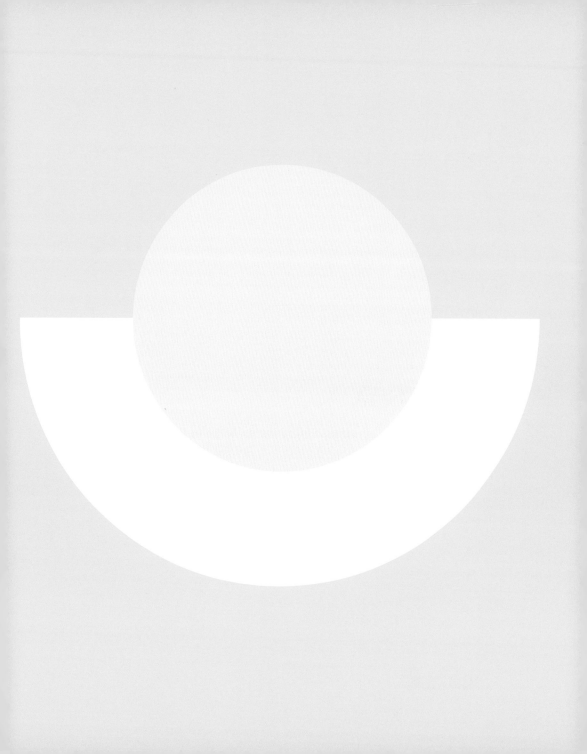

Pacifism.

In ethics or politics, an opposition to war or violence. This ranges from advocacy of peaceful solutions to problems, to a stance where all violence or force is considered morally wrong.

Pantheism.

The view that nature and God are the same thing; that everything in the universe is of an all-encompassing God.

Perspectivism.

Philosophical view that all ideas come from different perspectives and are caused by specific inner drives, and that any ethical judgement can be made from any number of viewpoints.

Pessimism.

A state of mind in which one believes only the worst to be possible; the philosophical view that the world is as bad as can be.

144 ▲

→ 136

Phenomenalism.

The view that physical things do not exist as things in themselves, but as a set of sensory stimuli that we experience or perceive.

Pluralism.

A philosophy which acknowledges the diversity of views within any given field, and seeks to accommodate these different views all at once.

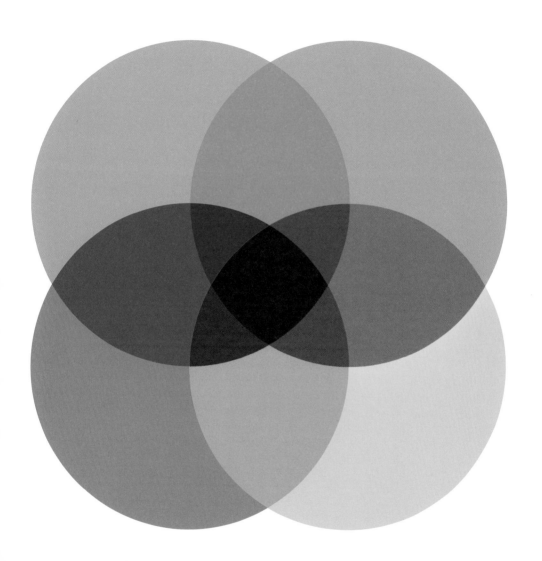

Positivism.

The position that the only authentic knowledge is that acquired through scientific means.

Pragmatism.

The view that practicality should be a vital component of meaning and truth, and that practice and theory should be linked.

Rationalism.

The theory that human reason can be the source of all knowledge.

154 ◻
→ 66

Realism.

The philosophical view that asserts that reality is fundamentally based on, and shaped by, ideas and mental experience, rather than material forces.

Reconstructivism.

A philosophy that holds that societies should continually reform in order to establish a more perfect government or social network.

Reductionism.

The idea that the nature of complex things can always be reduced and explained by simpler, more fundamental truths.

Relativism.

The assertion that no belief can be said to have absolute truth, having value only within a certain context or frame of reference.

162 □

→ 8

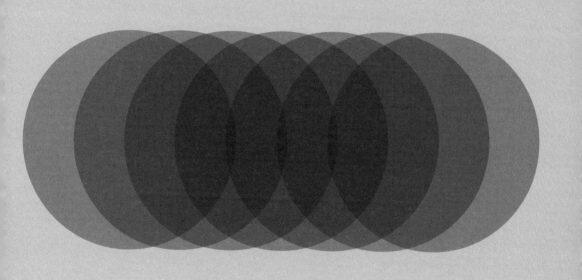

Secularism.

The idea that bodies of government should be completely separate from religious institutions.

Skepticism.

The method of practicing doubt when regarding what is held as knowledge.

Socialism.

An economic system in which the means of production
are owned and controlled by the many rather than the few.

Solipsism.

The view that only direct mental experience is certain,
as things external to one's own mind cannot be known.

Spiritualism.

The belief that spirits of the dead can be contacted through certain mediums, and that the guidance of the dead can be of spiritual value.

Stoicism.

The principle that emotional and physical self-control leads to inner peace and strength, allowing one to live a happier life.

Structuralism.

The theory that individual phenomena cannot be understood
except through understanding the wider structure, or context,
of their interrelations.

Subjectivism.

The view that one's own mind is the only unquestionable proof of existence, and that subjective experience is the root of all meaning in the world.

Symbolism.

The practice of using something (such as an image, symbol or word) to mean something other than itself.

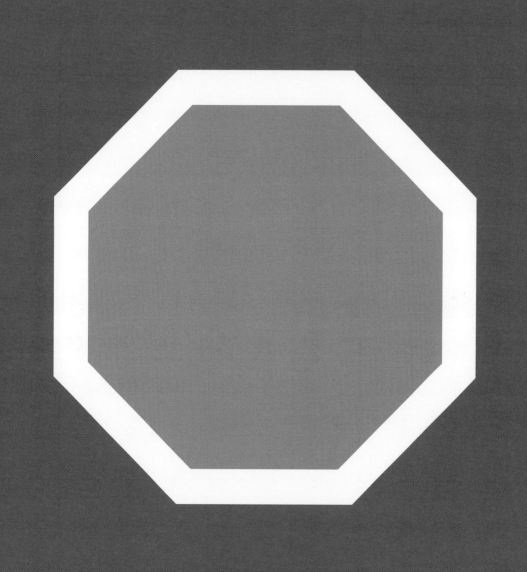

Syncretism.

The attempt to reconcile disparate, even contradictory, beliefs into one belief structure.

Theism.

The belief that a god or deity is present and active in the universe.

→ 22

Totalitarianism.

A political ideology in which a state enforces national loyalty
and identity in order to mobilise or oppress its population.

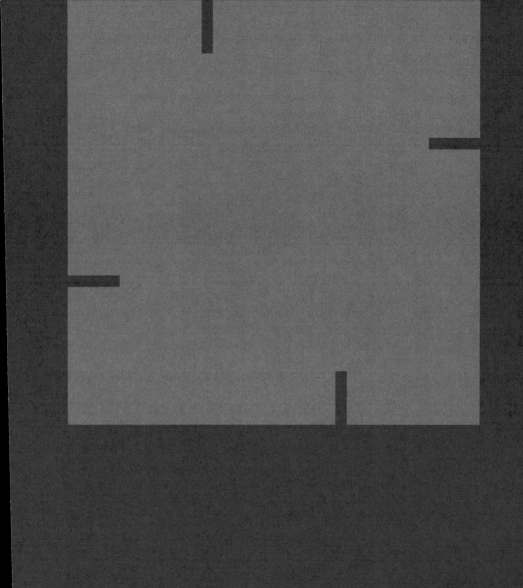

Transhumanism.

A movement supporting the use of new technology to enhance human potential, and eliminate undesirable aspects of the human condition, such as suffering, disease and ageing.

Universalism.

The belief that there are philosophical concepts that have universal application and relevance.

Utilitarianism.

The school of ethics that strives towards the maximisation of welfare for the maximum number of people.

Utopia.

The many various social and political movements based upon
the idea that paradise is achievable on earth.

Vitalism.

The doctrine that "vital forces", often equated with the soul, are active in living organisms, and that life cannot be explained solely by material or mechanism.

196 ▲
→ 108

Index

Acknowledgments

This book has been possible thanks to the contribution and advice of a bunch of individuals, and this is my chance to thank them.

To Chris Thomas, for his admirable task of boiling down and writing the concise definitions of this book.

To Martin Amor, for helping me find the direction on this project. To James Smith, the tutor who guided me on the early stages and en-couraged me to go further, abandon my comfort zone and find a new visual style.

To Rudolf van Wezel from BIS publisher, who believed in my idea and helped me to improve the outcome.

And to all the backers who supported this project when it was nothing more than an idea, who helped me self-publish the first edition of this book and who without their help this book would not exist.

Finally, thanks to my family, girlfriend and friends for always being there.